The Lost Bark

The Lost Bark

Poppy O'Neill

Mariano Epelbaum

Collins

Contents

Twiggy and Rafferty's house

farm

Chapter 1

The postman hadn't even reached the door before Twiggy began to bark. The soft crunch of his boots on the driveway was enough to wake her from her morning nap, with her ears pricked and tail pointing upwards.

Rafferty huffed and snuggled back into his bed. He'd never been that noisy when he was a puppy, he was sure of it.

"Be quiet, Twiggy," said the humans, all at once.

A handful of letters dropped onto the welcome mat, and Twiggy picked one up between her teeth, her tail wagging like a windscreen wiper.

"I'll take that," said Mum, gently sliding the letter out from between Twiggy's teeth. She gave a disgruntled "woof" and joined Rafferty by the radiator.

"I don't know why you're in such a good mood, Twiggy. Do you know what tonight is?" Rafferty stretched and rubbed his face against the soft fabric of his bed.

Twiggy cocked her head to the side. "I haven't a clue. Why?"

Rafferty looked fearfully at the window and said in a hushed voice, "Tonight is what the humans call Firework Night."

Twiggy didn't like the sound of that. Her ears flattened against her head and a soft "woof" escaped from her mouth. "What is a Fire Work?"

"A firework is a bright flash in the sky and a huge, terrifying boom." Rafferty's eyes widened. "It's the worst night of the year."

Twiggy's ears twitched back and forth. She barked at the window. "But why?"

"No dog knows why the humans have fireworks," said Rafferty. "They seem to like it, the strange creatures. Perhaps it's because of their small, hairless ears: they don't hear things like we do."

Twiggy stood up, her legs straight as pencils. "I won't let Firework Night happen." She barked at the window again, then scampered over to Mama, Mum, Lucy and Jack.

The humans had their coats on and were leaving for school and work. Twiggy woofed at each of them in turn. "No fireworks!" she barked. But the humans just ruffled her ears and told her to be quiet.

Ready for the day, the humans filed out of the front door, waving goodbye to Rafferty and Twiggy. Twiggy's tail gave a slow wag goodbye and she barked at the door as it closed.

All morning, Twiggy paced back and forth. *The worst night of the year* – Rafferty's words rang in her ears.

At lunch time, Mum came home to take Twiggy and Rafferty for a walk. The sound of her key in the front door made Twiggy jump. She barked in fear.

"Be quiet, Twiggy!" said Mum, shaking her head.

As they walked down the street they could smell that the other animals were worrying too. The birds were adding extra moss to their nests, and the badgers had already gone to bed, deep under the ground.

"I will bark at them," said Twiggy.

Rafferty cocked his head to one side. "At who?"

"At the fireworks!" yipped Twiggy. "I'll go into the garden and I'll bark and bark until the fireworks are scared of us instead."

Rafferty flicked his ears back. "You mustn't go into the garden on Firework Night!" he said urgently. He looked at Mum, then back to Twiggy. "I'm going to tell you a secret."

Twiggy padded over the grass to Rafferty, intrigued.

Rafferty looked from side to side. "Mum mustn't find out. Promise?"

Twiggy lifted her paw. "I promise."

"You know we're not allowed upstairs?"

"Oh yes, upstairs is just for humans," nodded Twiggy.

"On Firework Night, Mama lets me upstairs. I'm sure she'll let you, too."

Twiggy's eyes widened and her mouth fell open.

"Not just upstairs, but into Mama and Mum's bedroom and under their bed," Rafferty went on. "It's dark and soft – a good place to hide from the fireworks."

Twiggy couldn't believe her ears. When she was a tiny puppy, she'd run upstairs when the humans weren't looking, and done a wee on Lucy's carpet. That was the only time she'd been upstairs – it was a fascinating place, full of smells and soft things she'd like to nap on.

Mum looked at her watch – it was nearly time to go. She clipped Rafferty's lead onto his collar, and Twiggy's lead onto her harness.

"So you see," said Rafferty, "you mustn't go into the garden tonight. It could be dangerous, and I don't want to have to come out from under Mama and Mum's bed to rescue you."

Twiggy stopped to sniff an interesting piece of rubbish on the ground. She thought for a moment. Going upstairs did sound exciting, and a place to hide from the fireworks might be less scary than barking at them. She didn't want Mum to find out Mama and Rafferty's secret, either.

By the time they got home, Twiggy had made her decision.

The house

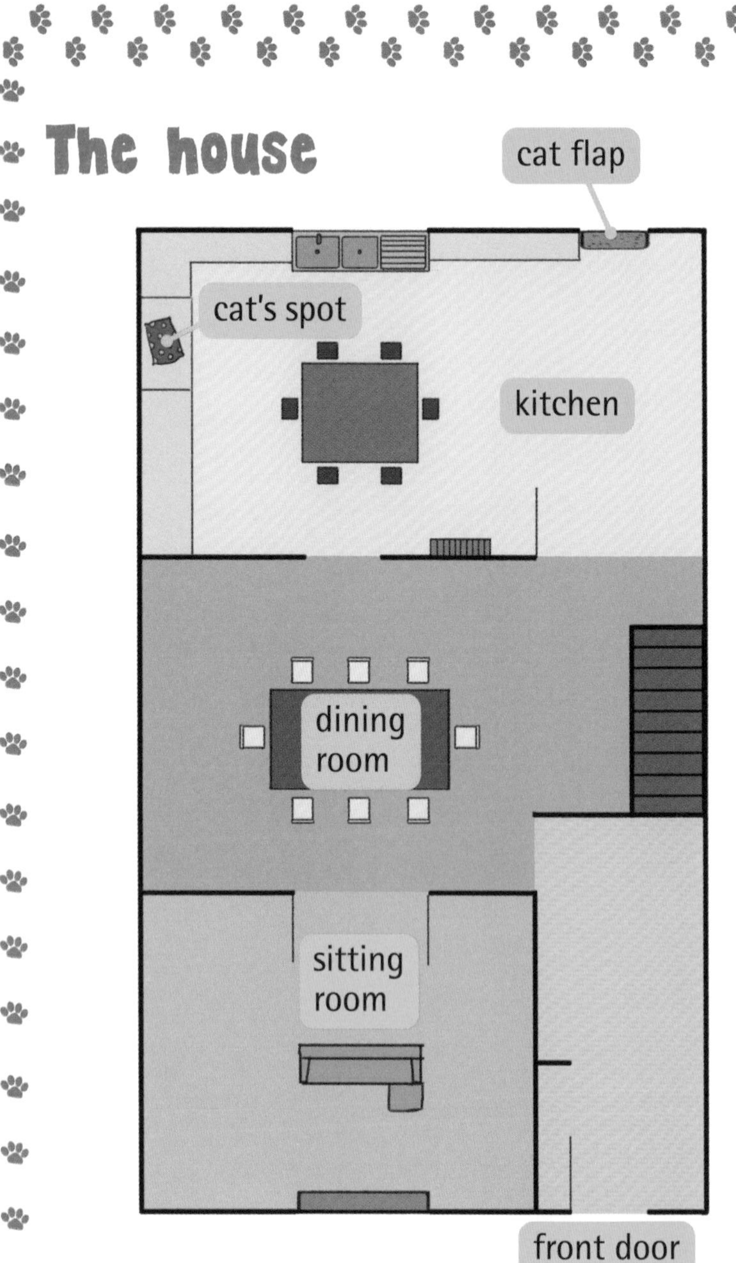
cat flap
cat's spot
kitchen
dining room
sitting room
front door

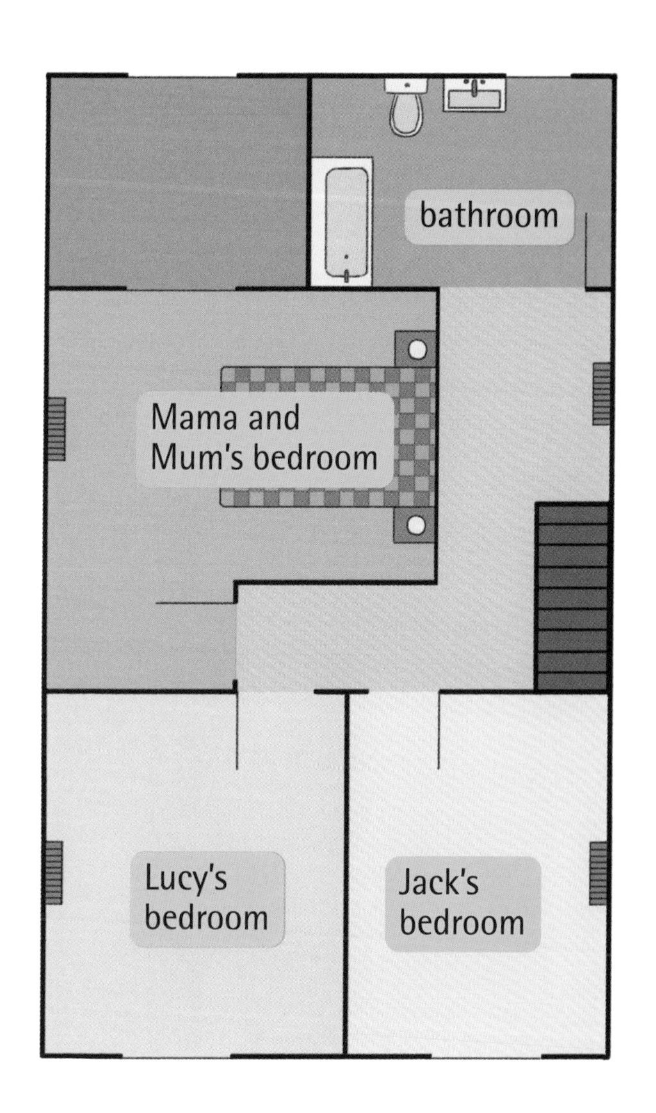
bathroom
Mama and
Mum's bedroom
Lucy's
bedroom
Jack's
bedroom

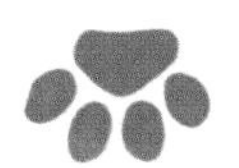

Chapter 2

As the sun set, Twiggy couldn't sit still. She picked up her cuddly duck toy and shook it from side to side in agitation. Rafferty was sitting bolt upright, unable to relax. Ginger, the family cat, came in through the cat flap earlier than usual and hid on top of the fridge. At last, Mama stuck her head round the door and motioned for the dogs to follow her.

The stair carpet felt soft and strange under Twiggy's paws, and she felt like barking to show her excitement. She made sure she stayed quiet though, wagging her tail vigorously instead.

Under Mama and Mum's bed, Mama had put cushions and her old dressing gown for Rafferty and Twiggy to lie on. The curtains were drawn and the radio was playing classical music on a low volume.

Rafferty snuggled down, relaxing into the dressing gown, which smelt like a warm hug from Mama. Twiggy padded over and nestled in beside Rafferty. Mama put her finger to her lips as she slipped out of the room, closing the door behind her.

"Have the fireworks started yet?" said Twiggy. But Rafferty was already snoring. If they had started, then this was a brilliant hiding place – she couldn't hear anything at all. The soft dressing gown, mixed with the sound of Rafferty's snores, made her feel sleepy. Her eyes slowly drooped closed.

Fizzzzz! Wooooo! Crrrrr!

A gigantic noise and a bright purple flash broke through the gap between the curtains, and Twiggy's eyes shot open. Rafferty groaned and hid his ears under his front paws. The noises were so loud that Twiggy couldn't hear her own thoughts. All she could hear were the fireworks, and all she could feel was fear.

Quick as lightning, Twiggy ran out from under the bed, through the door and down the stairs, barking with every step.

The humans were leaving the house, and they all turned to see Twiggy, fast and noisy as a firework herself, streak down the stairs and out of the front door.

Rafferty skidded to a halt at the top of the stairs, and Mum's forehead creased up in confusion. "How did you dogs get up there?"

In the cold of the garden, Twiggy looked up, terrified, at the brightly-lit sky. The fireworks whistled and boomed, cracked and wailed. She wished she had stayed under Mama and Mum's bed, safe and warm with Rafferty. Her bravery felt very small now that she was out in the garden by herself. Her legs shook and she mustered all her courage to bark at the noisy, naughty fireworks.

She wanted to bark "Leave us alone!" and "Be quiet!" and "You're scaring Rafferty!"

But when she opened her mouth, no bark came out.

She tried again, summoning a bark from deep within her belly, but all that came out was a high-pitched whimper. *I've lost my bark!* she thought, her stomach churning with confusion.

In a panic, Twiggy tore back into the house. She jumped up, scrambling at Mama's legs in fear. "Stay in the house," she wanted to bark, "or the fireworks will take your voices too!"

But Lucy and Jack just laughed and scruffled her fur.

"Why so quiet, Twiggy?" said Mum.

Twiggy looked up the stairs to Rafferty. She opened her mouth to bark. Rafferty watched, waiting for the familiar "woof" to escape Twiggy's mouth. But no sound came out. His ears pricked with delight – peace and quiet at last!

Pyooooooo! Krrrrreeee! A firework lit up the hallway and Rafferty's ears shot back in fright.

"Come on then, let's go and watch," said Mama.

"In your beds, Raff and Twiggy," said Mum. "No more going upstairs – you'll be OK."

The humans filed out of the front door, leaving the two dogs looking at each other. Rafferty turned towards Mama and Mum's room.

Twiggy whimpered and scratched at the bottom stair.

Rafferty stopped. "What is it?"

"We need to find my bark!" whispered Twiggy. "It went up with the fireworks and I'm going to get it back."

"No, Twiggy," said Rafferty. "Let's just get comfortable and wait for the fireworks to finish. Your bark will come back on its own, I'm sure."

The front door had been left slightly ajar, and Twiggy nosed it open. "It won't," she said in a quiet, raspy voice. "Wherever the fireworks are coming from, that's where I'll find my bark." With that, she disappeared out of the front door.

Rafferty huffed. He wanted to snuggle in Mama's dressing gown, but he wouldn't be able to relax if Twiggy was outside with the fireworks whizzing and crashing in the sky. Reluctantly, Rafferty bumped down the stairs, across the hall carpet and into the front garden.

It was dark, and the humans were holding sparkling sticks in their hands. By the sparkling light, he saw Twiggy sniffing something on the lawn.

Fireworks Night

Fireworks Night, also called Bonfire Night happens every year on November 5th in the UK.

People attend fireworks events and bonfires.

The reason is to remember a plot to blow up the king in the Houses of Parliament with gunpowder in 1605. The plot failed and so people celebrate that the king wasn't killed.

A lot of dogs and other animals don't like the noise and some pets get frightened and run away.

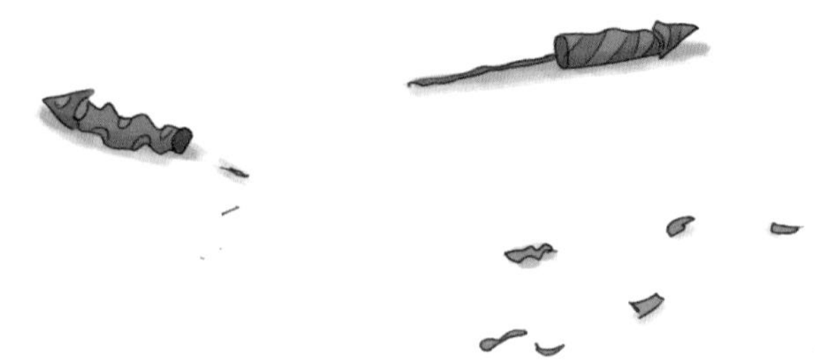

Chapter 3

"What is it?" Rafferty padded over the grass to see what Twiggy was sniffing. "It must be from the fireworks," he said, sniffing the object. "It doesn't smell like anything from our garden, or our neighbourhood. I can smell more of them in that direction."

Twiggy nodded, pointing her snout towards the side gate, beyond which lay fields that Mama and Mum said they weren't allowed to explore. "The fireworks took my bark and left us this, as a clue."

The object was a collection of cardboard tubes wrapped in colourful paper. Rafferty gave it another good sniff and sighed. "OK, Twiggy. I know your bark is very important to you. Mine is to me, though I only use it in emergencies."

The dogs sniffed the object again. They traced the smell of it across the lawn, through the slats of the gate and smelt how it had zoomed over the stony fields, leaving its scent stretching into the distance.

Rafferty looked back at the humans, who were still playing with their sparkling sticks. "I know a way through the hedge, Twiggy. Follow me."

Sliding under the hedge and through the gap in the fence, Rafferty sniffed for any dangers on the other side.

He smelt all the neighbourhood dogs and cats that had passed that spot. He smelt the humans and the different types of dirt that had been on the soles of their boots. He could smell the road, the tractor tyres that had rolled along it, and the fields beyond the road. Above it all, he could smell fireworks.

Twiggy followed Rafferty, rumpling her nose at the strong smell of fox that lingered on the crumbling soil. Fireworks banged and whooshed upwards from gardens and fields all around, startling them and making them jump and tremble every few steps.

Swiftly and carefully, the two dogs scurried across the quiet road. Rafferty's nose picked up the scent of the fireworks like a trail across the ground. Twiggy caught the scent too, and together they followed it onto the field, their strong, quick paws leaving prints in the earth.

A firework lit up the sky directly above them with a huge bang. Twiggy's tail curled downwards, and Rafferty let out a yelp. He shook himself, briskly shaking the fear out of his body. The noise had faded but Twiggy stood as still as a statue.

"You need to shake," said Rafferty, "otherwise the fear stays inside you."

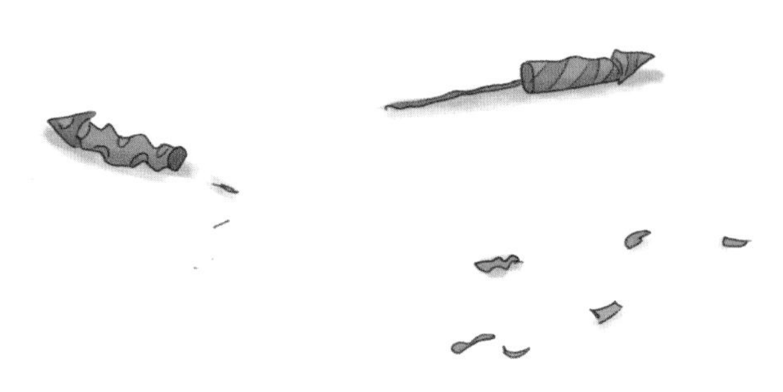

Twiggy started with her ears, shaking her head from side to side so they flapped against each other. Rafferty was right, it did feel better. She let her shoulders jiggle and her back legs wiggle, feeling the fear fading and her bravery return.

"Good," said Rafferty, "now let's keep going."

But Twiggy hesitated.

"You're worried about Mama and Mum. They're having fun with the fireworks – they'll think we're in our beds already," Rafferty reassured her. "We just need to find your bark and then we'll run straight back. The firework smell is getting stronger, we must be nearly there."

Twiggy looked back towards their house and saw the faint glow of the humans and their sparkling sticks in the garden. She wanted to bark so Mama and Mum would come and get her. But they'd be so cross if they knew. She sniffed the ground. Rafferty was right, the firework smell was tingling in her nostrils now, pulling her away from home and towards a large building at the edge of the field. She turned and started padding forwards.

When they reached the building, the dogs sniffed the cold bricks – they smelt all kinds of animals: chickens, cows, horses.

Twiggy sniffed again and looked confused.

"It's a farm," said Rafferty wisely. He'd been past this place in the car, his head sticking out of the window.

They drew their noses close to the fence around the farmyard, sniffing for a way in. Rafferty knew it was always a good idea to sniff for fox smells, because foxes are experts at getting through fences.

After a while, they found a gap in the fence next to the building and squeezed through. The smell of fireworks filled Twiggy's nostrils, a hundred times stronger than it had been in the field. She could smell all the materials they were made of – wood, cardboard, paper, and the powder that she guessed caused the terrible noises.

They were in a large, square farmyard surrounded by barns and buildings. There was a house with lights on in some of the windows, and Twiggy wondered if there was a family of humans like hers inside, getting ready for bed and cuddling their dogs goodnight.

Rafferty could see Twiggy's bravery wavering. "Follow me." He pointed his snout towards the corner of the farmyard, and they padded quietly across the ground.

Lucy's diary

Dear Diary,

It's quite late now so I won't write much. This morning I got woken up by Twiggy barking again! I wish she knew how to tell the time – I like to stay asleep as long as possible, especially on a school day. I hope as she gets older that she quietens down a bit. At least it's Saturday tomorrow – no school!

I felt really sorry for the pets when the fireworks started. Ginger doesn't seem to mind – nothing bothers Ginger – but Rafferty gets really frightened and it was Twiggy's first firework night. She came running out of the front door to see what was going on! Brave little girl.

We had sparklers in the garden and watched the fireworks being launched from other people's gardens. The farm across the way always has a big display. I wonder how their animals feel about it. We got really cold out in the garden but it was good fun. The dogs must have put themselves to bed as we didn't see them when we came inside.

Lucy

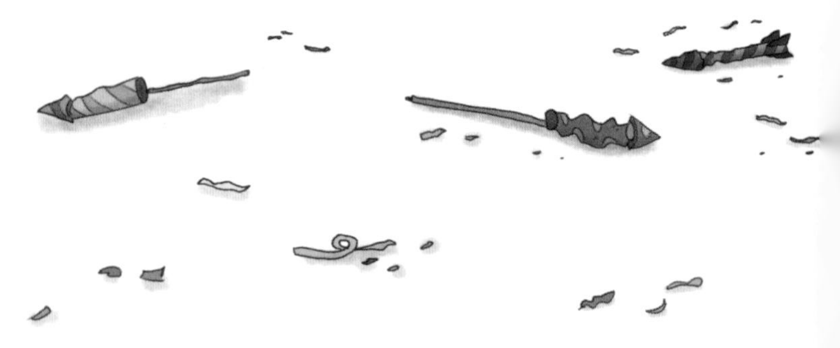

Chapter 4

As they came closer, Twiggy could see objects like the one in their own garden all over the ground. There was a fire still softly smouldering, and the remains of a dozen sparkling sticks stood drowned in a bucket of sand. She knew now that these were fireworks that had lost their bangs. She smelt each one in turn, her tail wagging with hope.

Rafferty nervously scratched his shoulder with his back leg. "Have you found it?" he said.

Twiggy shrugged. She thought she'd be able to smell her bark, to find it like they'd found the fireworks. But maybe her bark didn't have a smell.

"Give it a try," Rafferty urged her.

Twiggy stood as tall as her little legs could make her, drew up all the bravery in her heart and opened her mouth.

But no sound came out.

Twiggy felt scared. Instead of hope, the smell of the fireworks now filled her with dread. What if she never barked again? How would she show her humans that she was happy to see them, or that there was a squirrel in the garden, or that someone was at the door?

A howl escaped Rafferty's mouth. He'd thought their plan would work, and that they'd be tucked up in their beds by the radiator in the kitchen by now. He worried that they'd never find Twiggy's bark, and that she'd feel scared and sad forever without it. The two dogs huddled together in the cold farmyard, wondering what to do next.

From the glow of the house came a noise that made Twiggy and Rafferty's fur stand on end. A growl, followed by a series of loud barks. The barks said: "This is our home. Go away!"

Looking around in a panic for somewhere to hide, Twiggy spotted an open barn door. The two dogs dashed into the darkness of the barn.

It was filled with the smell of sheep, foxes, cats and chickens. As his eyes grew accustomed to the lack of light, Rafferty saw why so many animals had passed through the barn: it was filled from floor to ceiling with warm, dry hay.

Twiggy sniffed the big golden bricks of dried grass, feeling suddenly very tired. She couldn't find her bark anywhere. It seemed like the barking dogs were staying inside the house, so maybe she and Rafferty could rest here for a little while, and sneak home after a nap. Maybe she'd find her bark in among the hay and the animal smells.

As soon as Twiggy started to relax, they heard the sound of someone opening the door of the house and some barking. A human voice said, "Be quiet, Buster!" and the noise of the barking grew closer, followed by large paws bounding across the farmyard.

Terrified, Twiggy and Rafferty scrambled onto a bale of hay. They could hear Buster sniffing loudly, and they could smell that he didn't want them in this barn. Twiggy and Rafferty lay down very quietly next to each other, their ears pinned close to their heads, barely daring to breathe.

Buster was soon joined by two other large dogs, and together they strode into the barn. Twiggy had never heard barking so loud or growling so scary. She didn't want to bark back, even if she could. It made her head hurt and her heart beat fast. She buried her face in the tickly hay and snuggled closer to Rafferty.

After what felt like a million years of barking, one of the humans came to fetch the big dogs, and they trotted obediently back into the house, throwing a couple of "woofs" towards the barn on their way.

Trembling, Twiggy lifted her face. Her fur was scruffy and full of little bits of hay.

Rafferty stood up and shook the fear out of him. "Come on, Twiggy, shake it off," he said.

But Twiggy laid still. "Those dogs *really* want us to leave," she whispered. "They were so noisy."

"Yes," said Rafferty. "This is their home, and they don't understand why we're here."

"Do you think they know where my bark is?" Twiggy wondered.

"I don't think they'd tell us, even if they did know," said Rafferty.

Twiggy's chin dropped onto her paws.

At the sight of Twiggy so forlorn, Rafferty snuggled in close to her and licked her soft, furry head. "Your bark is part of what makes you special," he said. "It's how you say 'hello' and how you show your feelings. Your bark is important to you, and you're important to me."

Twiggy sniffled. Through the barn door she could see the stars twinkling in the dark, quiet sky. She wondered what the stars smelt like, and she wondered if she'd ever bark again.

Dog powers

Just like Rafferty and Twiggy, real dogs have strong senses and great skills.

Emotional intelligence – for spotting behaviour and scent cues about how animals and humans are feeling

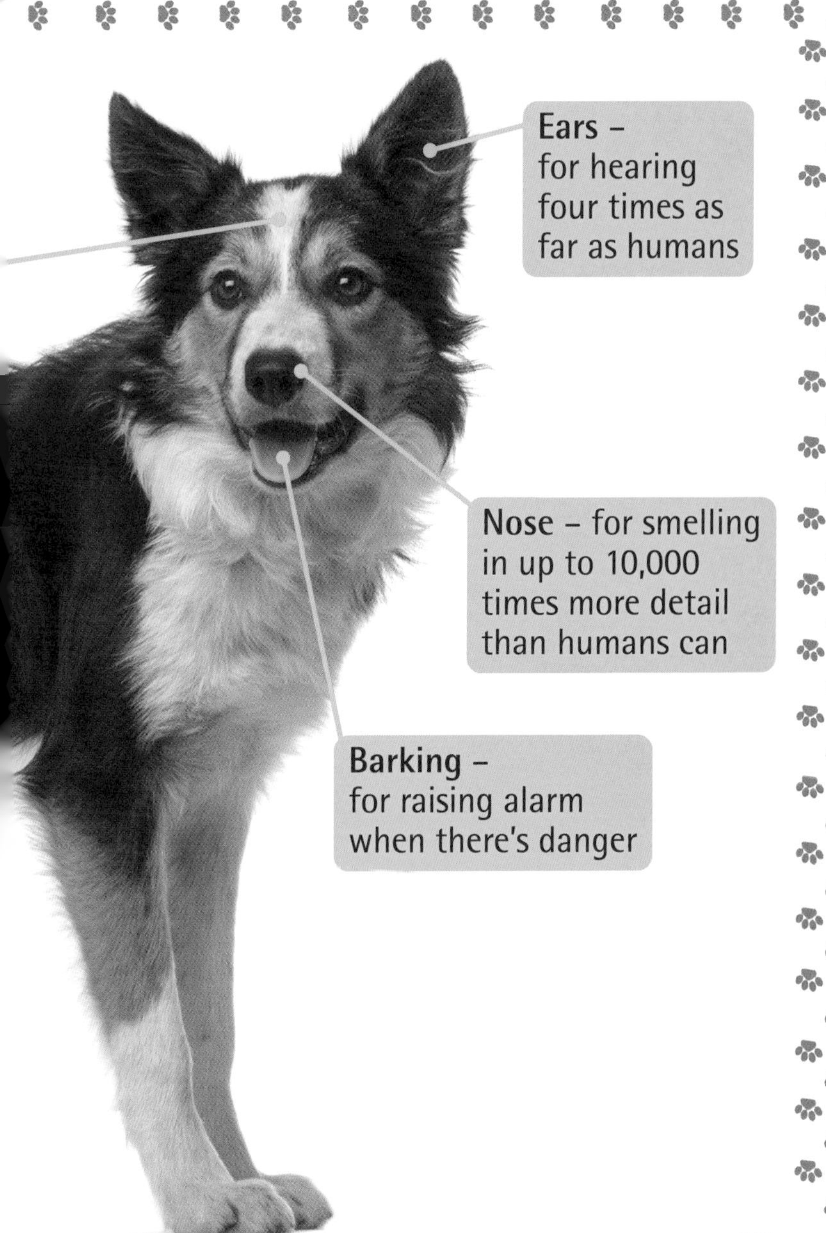
Ears –
for hearing
four times as
far as humans
Nose – for smelling
in up to 10,000
times more detail
than humans can
Barking –
for raising alarm
when there's danger

Chapter 5

The dogs lay on top of the hay bale a little longer in silence. They wanted to be sure that Buster and his friends weren't coming back outside.

Feeling brave, Twiggy lifted her head. She hadn't heard a bark or a firework for ages. She nuzzled Rafferty, trying to get him to stand up with her.

"But we haven't found your bark," said Rafferty.

Twiggy let out a soft howl in the direction of their home. She missed her humans, and both dogs knew that the longer they were away, the more likely that the humans would notice they were gone.

The thought of Mama, Mum, Lucy and Jack filled Rafferty's heart with longing. He'd never been away from home for this long. He nodded in agreement. "Let's go home."

Easily springing from bale to bale, Twiggy started to make her way down. But for Rafferty, his older legs made the climb trickier, and each bale wobbled underneath him as he tried to steady himself.

"Twiggy, slow down!" he called softly, and just as she turned her head up and around to see him, he disappeared between two bales of hay.

Twiggy sprung back up to where Rafferty had fallen. It was very dark and she couldn't see him, but she could smell his familiar scent. She heard Rafferty give a high-pitched bark. She could hear how frightened he was, and she knew she had to rescue him.

Sniffing the hay for the best place to dig, Twiggy moved quickly. She wanted more than anything to give a reassuring bark, so that Rafferty knew she was on her way.

A patch at the edge of one of the hay bales closest to the ground smelt soft and crumbly enough, and Twiggy began to dig. She moved her paws at a furious speed and put all her strength into her sturdy front legs.

After what felt like forever, her front paws broke through and she felt Rafferty's rough fur against the pads of her feet. "Follow me!" she said, wriggling backwards through the cramped tunnel she'd dug.

Rafferty was panting with fear, and he crawled after her, thankful for his brave friend.

They emerged into the cold, quiet barn and stopped for a moment to catch their breath.

"You were really brave," he said. "Thank you for rescuing me."

"It's what friends are for," said Twiggy. Just then, her ears pricked up at the sound of birdsong.

The two dogs looked at the horizon – the sun's rays were beginning to glow above the trees in the distance, and they could see the chimney of their home. It was time to go.

The farmyard had a grey tinge in the morning light. Twiggy and Rafferty squeezed through the gap in the fence and started out across the field. They didn't need to sniff to find their way, and neither spoke as they trudged across the stony ground.

As they approached the road between the field and their house, Twiggy stopped. Rafferty looked over his shoulder at her, raising one paw from the ground.

Just one last try, Twiggy thought. She stood as tall as she could, her four paws firmly rooted. She raised her face to the rising sun and willed a bark to emerge from her mouth. But still, no bark came. She dropped her head downwards. She had failed.

Rafferty gave a low howl of sympathy. The two dogs stood a few moments longer at the edge of the field, not knowing what to do. The house would be very different without Twiggy's bark.

A lonely car rolled along the road.

"Come on, let's go," said Rafferty, once it had passed.

Twiggy nodded, and they trotted across the cold tarmac, through the hedge and into their garden.

The sun shone a sliver of light along the very edge of the lawn, and the grass between the dogs and the house sparkled with frost. Exhausted, Twiggy and Rafferty padded towards the back door.

Twiggy opened her mouth out of habit. Then she realised. "How will we get in without waking up Mama and Mum? They'll know we were gone."

Rafferty looked around, checking the cat wasn't watching. "I'm not proud of this," he said, "but I have something to show you."

Twiggy watched, her eyes widening with surprise, as Rafferty nosed open the cat flap. He drew his shoulder blades together and slid the front half of his body through the small hole. Then, he carefully lifted one leg at a time, disappearing into the house.

A moment later, he poked his head back through the cat flap. "Now you try," he said sheepishly.

"I'm astonished," whispered Twiggy. "First Mama and Mum's bed, now this!"

Rafferty laughed, and for the first time since he'd told Twiggy about fireworks, the two dogs felt happy.

Rafferty ducked back inside the house, and Twiggy wriggled after him.

Rafferty and Twiggy

Rafferty

Wisdom: **10**

Grumpiness: **8**

Friendship: **10**

Speed: **3**

Twiggy

Wisdom: 4

Grumpiness: 0

Friendship: 10

Speed: 8

Chapter 6

Everything was very still inside the kitchen. On top of the fridge, the cat lifted her head at the sound of the cat flap, rolled her eyes and went straight back to sleep.

The dogs could see last night's washing up by the kitchen sink, and the door to the cupboard where the treats and dog food was kept. The room smelt gloriously of home, of family and safety and love.

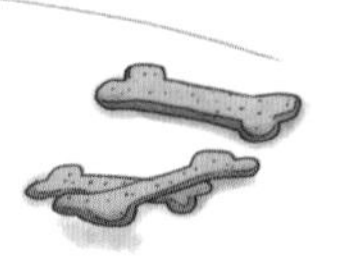

The dogs' beds were where they always were, next to the radiator. They looked softer and comfier than ever, and Twiggy collapsed onto hers, her chin resting on the squishy, cushioned side.

"Just one more thing before we sleep," said Rafferty.

Twiggy whined and yawned.

"We've done lots of scary things tonight," Rafferty said, coaxing Twiggy out of her bed. "What do we do after we get scared?"

Twiggy thought for a moment. She wriggled her shoulders to show Rafferty she understood.

"That's right," said Rafferty, and he shook himself from his ears to the tip of his tail.

Twiggy did the same, her paws skidding on the smooth tiled floor as she wriggled and shook herself from nose to tail. She felt a mixture of sadness for her bark, and relief at being home after what felt like the longest night of her life. She snuggled back into her bed.

Rafferty stepped into his bed, exhaling heavily. He didn't know what the house would be like without Twiggy's bark. She'd been part of his family for less than a year, but already it felt strange to think of life without a bright, joyful "woof" to punctuate the day.

"Goodnight, Twiggy," he said softly.

"Goodnight, Rafferty."

For a moment, they were both quiet.

"Rafferty?" said Twiggy.

"Yes?"

"Do you think the humans will still love me without my bark?" Twiggy's voice was shaking.

Rafferty raised himself up from his bed and shifted over to join Twiggy in hers. It was a tight squeeze, and the dogs cuddled close around each other. Rafferty gave Twiggy's silky-soft ear a gentle lick.

"Of course they will," he said. "They'll love you no matter what."

Twiggy sighed with relief. Her eyelids began to droop closed.

Rafferty watched her fall asleep, then closed his eyes too.

As the dogs drifted off to sleep, the world outside the kitchen window was waking up. The sun rose higher in the clear morning sky, its warmth softening the frost that had grown on the hedgerows and the used fireworks overnight.

The door to the kitchen squeaked sharply as Mum bustled through it, looking for her favourite coffee cup.

Twiggy's ears pricked up and her eyes snapped open. She'd been dreaming of chasing quick foxes up and down soft hay bales.

At the sight of Mum, Twiggy leapt out of bed. She knelt down to ruffle her ears, pulling a piece of hay from her fur. Mum looked quizzically at the piece of hay, then at Twiggy. "You're very quiet, Twiggy."

She nuzzled her snout against Mum's leg, and Mum picked her up for a cuddle.

"Yesterday was your first firework night; it must have been scary for you," she said. "Maybe that's why you're not yourself."

Twiggy licked Mum's ear and laid her head on her shoulder. Her heart felt happy, and she gave a gentle "yip!"

Rafferty opened one eye in annoyance. Then, as memories of the night before came rushing back, he gave a yelp of surprise and delight.

Twiggy wagged her tail furiously. She barked again, louder this time and full of joy.

Mum laughed and placed Twiggy down on the floor.

"Woof!" she said, jumping and spinning around the kitchen.

"What's going on?" Lucy put her head around the door and grinned at Twiggy. "You're in a good mood!"

Jack's face appeared just below Lucy's. "Twiggy's dancing!" he exclaimed.

Just then, Mama came in through the back door, wearing her gardening gloves. "You're awake!"

Twiggy skipped over to Mama, tottering on her back legs and barking with all her might. Mama took her paws and they danced together, Twiggy's tongue hanging out of her mouth like a pink ribbon.

Rafferty tapped across the floor to Mum, and rubbed his snout against Mum's jeans. Mum reached down and scratched Rafferty behind his ears – Rafferty's favourite spot.

Mum made cups of hot chocolate and Mama lit the fire in the sitting room, and the whole family sat down to watch a film together.

The dogs got comfortable on the rug in front of the fire.

"I found my bark!" barked Twiggy, full to the brim with happiness.

But Rafferty wasn't so sure. "Maybe it was never lost," he said. "Maybe it was just hiding."

Twiggy thought for a moment, then barked in agreement.

"Be quiet now, Twiggy, the film's starting," said Mama.

When it's hard to speak

For some people, when they feel very frightened or anxious, it's hard to talk. This can happen to people who find it easy to speak in situations where they feel comfortable and calm. Sometimes, this is called selective mutism or situational mutism.

How might selective mutism feel?

My tummy hurts.

I'm scared but
I don't know how
to ask for help.

Please don't ask
me to speak.

Talking feels
too difficult
right now.

I wish the grown-ups
around me understood, but
I can't tell them.

You can help

If someone is finding it difficult to speak, here's how you can support them and show them kindness.

- Reassure them that it's OK not to talk.
- Stay calm and friendly.
- Play a game together that doesn't involve talking.
- Sit quietly together.
- Use your voice to explain to a grown-up that your friend is finding it too difficult to speak.

About the author

A bit about me …

I've been an author for six years, it's what I've always wanted to be. I live in Sussex with my wife, children and our cats and dogs.

How did you get into writing?

I studied writing at university, and while I was there I met an editor from a local publisher. She was looking for new writers and gave me the opportunity to write a book for children about anxiety. It's all grown from there.

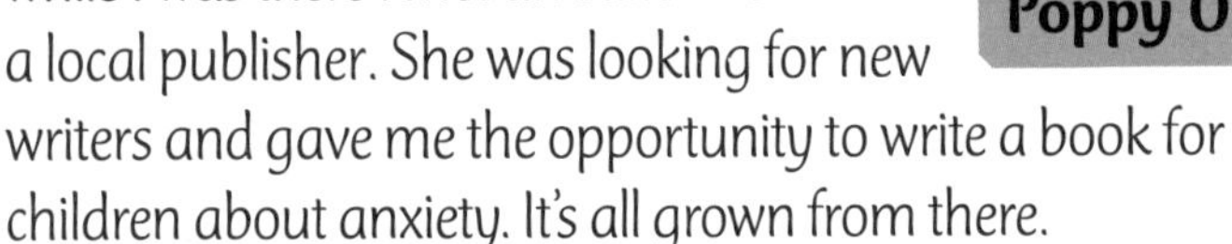

Poppy O'Neill

What do you hope readers will get out of the book?

First and foremost, I hope readers enjoy the book. I certainly enjoyed writing it. I also hope readers take a message from the book about fear and bravery – that they look different for everybody.

Is there anything in this book that relates to your own experiences?

A very brave boy I know sometimes struggles with speaking up. He inspired me to write the story.

What is it like for you to write?

I love writing. I like to plan what's going to happen in each chapter quite carefully first, so that I can enjoy writing without worrying the story will go too slowly or too fast, or veer off in a different direction.

What is a book you remember loving reading when you were young?
I loved *Matilda* by Roald Dahl, and the *Horrible History* book series.

Why did you want to write this book?
This is my first book where animals are the main characters, and I wanted to challenge myself to write from the point of view of a character that wasn't human.

What gave you the idea of writing about a dog who lost their bark?
I love how expressive dogs are, and how their barks are just one of many ways they communicate their emotions and opinions. I thought it was an interesting way to explore the feeling of fear and finding it difficult to talk.

Do you have a message for children who find it difficult to talk?
It's OK not to talk. It's really hard when people don't understand, and I hope your friends and grown-ups recognise how brave you are.

Do you own a dog? Are they like either of the dogs in this story?
Yes, Twiggy and Rafferty are based on my own dogs!

Do you have a top tip for dog-owners?
You can learn as much from your dog as they can from you.

About the illustrator

A bit about me

Hi, I'm Mariano, I'm from Buenos Aires, Argentina.

Mariano Epelbaum

What made you want to be an illustrator?

I believe I came to this world with a pencil! I was always drawing small insects in the garden at my grandmother's house and drawing characters and super-heroes during my childhood. I loved cartoons like *The Looney Tunes, Tex Avery and Disney*.

How did you get into illustration?

I started by designing a character for a Sports club and some spot illustrations for books. Then, I worked as an animator. I decided to develop my illustration style so I could work in books.

What did you like best about illustrating this book?

I enjoyed visualising the cute dogs in different situations and thinking about their behaviours, I love dogs!

Is there anything in this book that relates to your own experiences?

Oh yes, I suffered from being shy and introverted until I was about 17. The loneliness was hard!

How do you bring a character to life?

When possible, I draw several roughs poses and expressions trying to find the personality.

Do you find it fun to illustrate dogs?

I love dogs! My puppy, Flopi, is 4 months old and she has similar fur to Rafferty's so I enjoyed drawing the fur, even though it's quite hard. When you are an illustrator you are alone a lot of time so dogs are great company. It is quite important to have breaks and go for walks to the park to stay healthy.

How do you convey personality when you're drawing a dog?

Observing and remembering different situations with my pet and transforming all of these into body language and expressions.

When you're drawing animals, do you prefer to work from photos or from real life?

Photos are so important to analyse the shapes, sizes, poses, structure, all the necessary things for a good illustration. But real life gives you instant mental images, so I can work on rapid sketches to capture the character.

Book chat

Which character did you like best, and why?

Did your mood change while you were reading the book? If so, how?

If you could change one thing about this book, what would it be?

If you had to give the book a new title, what would you choose?

Which part of the book did you like best, and why?

Did this book remind you of anything you have experienced in real life?

Which scene stands out most for you? Why?

What do you think Twiggy and Rafferty learned through their experiences?

Book challenge:

Design an area for a pet to be cosy during Fireworks Night.

Published by Collins
An imprint of HarperCollins*Publishers*

The News Building
1 London Bridge Street
London SE1 9GF
UK

Macken House
39/40 Mayor Street Upper
Dublin 1
D01 C9W8
Ireland

10 9 8 7 6 5 4 3 2 1

ISBN 978-0-00-862482-8

British Library Cataloguing-in-Publication Data
A catalogue record for this publication is available from the British Library.

Download the teaching notes and word cards to accompany this book at:
http://littlewandle.org.uk/signupfluency/

Author: Poppy O'Neill
Illustrator: Mariano Epelbaum (Astound Illustration Agency)
Publisher: Lizzie Catford
Product manager and commissioning editor: Caroline Green
Series editor: Charlotte Raby
Development editor: Catherine Baker
Project manager: Emily Hooton
Content editor: Daniela Mora Chavarría
Copyeditor: Sally Byford
Proofreader: Gaynor Spry
Cover designer: Sarah Finan
Typesetter: 2Hoots Publishing Services Ltd
Production controller: Katharine Willard

Collins would like to thank the teachers and children at the following schools who took part in the trialling of Big Cat for Little Wandle Fluency: Burley And Woodhead Church of England Primary School; Chesterton Primary School; Lady Margaret Primary School; Little Sutton Primary School; Parsloes Primary School.

Printed and bound in the UK using 100% Renewable Electricity at Martins the Printers Ltd

MIX
Paper | Supporting responsible forestry
FSC™ C007454

This book is produced from independently certified FSC™ paper to ensure responsible forest management.

For more information visit: www.harpercollins.co.uk/green

Acknowledgements
The publishers gratefully acknowledge the permission granted to reproduce the copyright material in this book. Every effort has been made to trace copyright holders and to obtain their permission for the use of copyright material. The publishers will gladly receive any information enabling them to rectify any error or omission at the first opportunity.

pp30–31 Veganik/Shutterstock, pp54–55 Eric Isselee/Shutterstock.